JOSHUA LAWRENCE CHAMBERLAIN

AMERICAN HERO

ROBERT F. KENNEDY, JR.

Illustrated by Nikita Andreev

Sky Pony Press
New York, NY

ACKNOWLEDGMENTS

My son Conor inspired me to write this book when he undertook a writing project on Joshua Chamberlain for his fifth grade history class at Brunswick School. Conor acted as my researcher, providing me with answers to every question I asked about Chamberlain and the various battles of the Civil War. I also want to gratefully acknowledge my friend Val Chamberlain, who provided a number of research articles for this book.

Visit our website at www.skyponypress.com.
Please follow our publisher Tony Lyons on Instagram @tonylyonsisuncertain

10 9 8 7 6 5 4 3 2 1

Library of Congress Cataloging-in-Publication Data is available on file.

Cover design by Kai Texel

Map of Gettysburg on page iv © Bettman/Corbis
Photograph on page vi © Corbis
Photograph on page viii by Jacques Lowe
Photograph on page 37 courtesy of Maine Historical Society

Sources for asterisked quotes are listed on page 38.

Print ISBN: 978-1-5107-7904-4
Ebook ISBN: 978-1-5107-7957-0

Manufactured in China, August 2023
This product conforms to CPSIA 2008

To the courageous men and women of America's armed forces
—R.F.K., Jr.

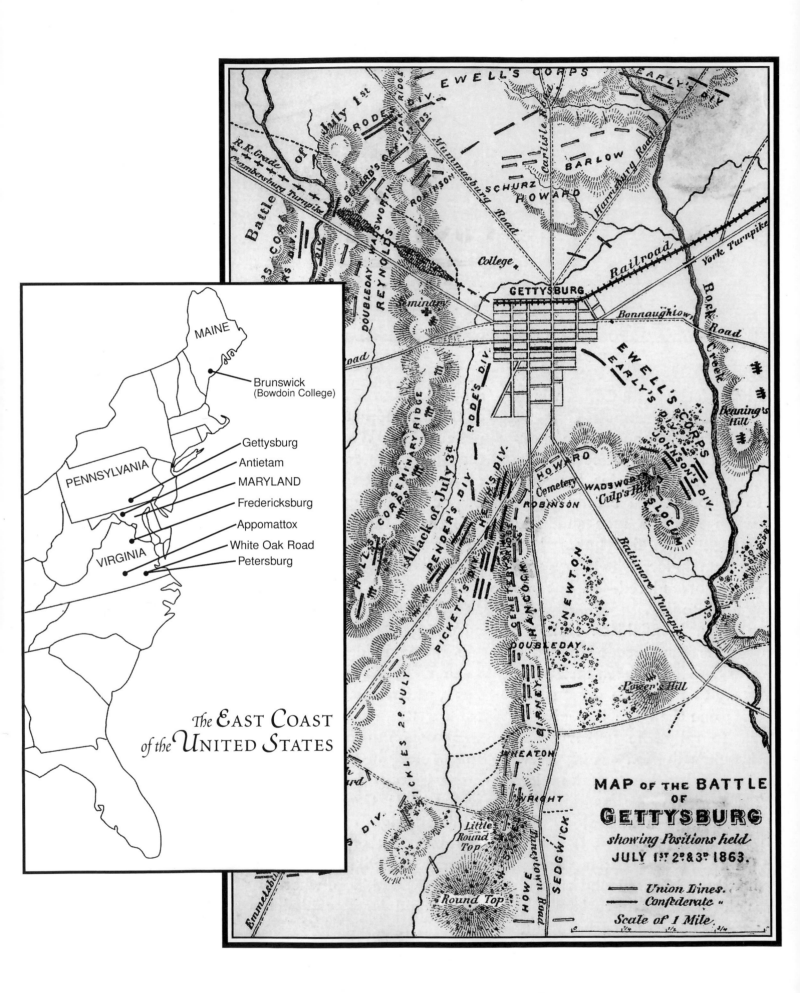

The EAST COAST of the UNITED STATES

MAINE

Brunswick
(Bowdoin College)

Gettysburg
Antietam
MARYLAND
Fredericksburg
Appomattox
White Oak Road
Petersburg

PENNSYLVANIA

VIRGINIA

MAP of the BATTLE
OF
GETTYSBURG
showing Positions held
JULY 1ST 2ND & 3RD 1863.

Union Lines.
Confederate "

Scale of 1 Mile.

CONTENTS

Joshua Chamberlain, circa 1864

FOREWORD

Sometimes the fate of a nation rests upon the shoulders of a single courageous soul.

ONE DAY IN JULY 1863, a young college professor named Joshua Chamberlain and a handful of gallant boys from Maine risked—and in some cases, gave—their lives to hold a few acres of rough, rocky soil on a Pennsylvania hilltop. Their heroic deeds saved our country from destruction. Their legacy is the United States of America, and the courage, character, and goodness that make our country a great nation.

Had Chamberlain or his men faltered, even momentarily, during the fight for the Round Tops, our nation would have died at Gettysburg. After that battle, Chamberlain and the men of the 20th Maine buried their dead, side by side, in a single long grave. They memorialized each of their fallen comrades with a plank torn from an ammunition box and inscribed with the soldier's name. As he completed this grim task, Chamberlain wistfully hoped that generations of Americans who "know us not" would come from afar, "to see where and by whom great things were suffered and done for them."

I wrote this book in the hope that our children will put a higher value on America and its freedoms if they understand the high price at which these things were purchased by an earlier generation of our countrymen. The recitation of a glorious history and heroic deeds has the power to imbue us with noble thoughts and summons us to the ideals and courage that make America great.

In their efforts to improve our minds and elevate our souls, my parents encouraged their eleven children to read history and learn about the great heroes of the past. My father, an avid military historian, told us, over dinner, the stories of important battles like Bunker Hill, the Cowpens, and Bull Run. Our family visited the decisive battlefields of the Revolution and the Civil War. On one

The author as a child with his father

of these trips, to Gettysburg, we heard the story of the citizen soldier Joshua Chamberlain.

Chamberlain epitomized the best qualities of the American character. He was a hardworking farmer; a poet and a musician; a linguist, writer, and theologian. He was educated and idealistic. He was self-reliant, kind, fair, and decent. He had character, integrity, and manners. He loved America and was willing to sacrifice his life and fortune for our country. His astounding feats of daring in the nation's time of greatest peril compare with epic deeds of the warriors of ancient times and legend.

The extraordinary thing is how common these virtues were in so many of those who fought in the Civil War, on both sides. Indeed, the Civil War is the story of millions of acts of heartbreaking gallantry. Chamberlain and his contemporaries faced crises far more dire than any known to this generation. More than 620,000 American soldiers died in that conflict, a catastrophe equivalent to the loss of 5.7 million Americans relative to the country's population today. Our nation faced imminent destruction. Whole cities were besieged and ruined; our countryside was immolated; railroads and roads destroyed. Yet, the Americans fighting for the Union cause did not compromise their principles or their commitment to justice. They never dismissed their vision of a noble and just America as if it were a luxury that we could no longer afford. Their dauntlessness transformed the Civil War from America's gravest and most tragic episode into our country's finest hour. Its successful prosecution required great national sacrifice, the guidance of Providence, and extraordinary heroics by thousands of citizens, from President Lincoln to the lowest infantryman. Their efforts saved the Union and abolished slavery, which had torn the moral fiber of our young republic. They helped confirm America as the generous, principled nation we became in our own eyes—and in the eyes of the world. When he spoke of the war, Chamberlain referred to it, in the common parlance of the day, as "the noble cause." Chamberlain and his soldiers fought the war to preserve not just the solidarity but the virtues of our nation—our idealism, faith, optimism, decency, and commitment to justice. The most conspicuous quality of these men was courage.

In the view of earlier American generations, courage was practically synonymous with freedom; fear, after all, was the instrument of tyrants. As Franklin Roosevelt later put it, the greatest enemy of our treasured freedom is "fear itself." Every once in a while, we Americans need to remind ourselves that we are the land of the free precisely *because* we are the home of the brave! A nation of great ideals can be preserved only by sacrifice and courage. I grew up thinking of Americans as the bravest people on earth. Americans, our civics instructors taught us, were guided by principle and willing to sacrifice all to preserve our rights and liberty.

It is the fantastic bravery of a long line of stalwarts like Joshua Chamberlain, and their love of principle, their commitment to ideals, and their willingness to sacrifice, which has defined our people and guided our nation's destiny. It's worth considering today how grievously we would dishonor the memory of these gallant heroes if we should ever let America become a nation governed by fear, or if we willingly compromised the rights they gave so much to guarantee.

—*Robert F. Kennedy, Jr.*

1.

"JUST DO IT!"

◆——◆◇◆——◆

Joshua Chamberlain was born September 8, 1828, in Brewer, Maine, the oldest of five children. His parents required their children to be honest, honorable, and cheerful. Joshua had to practice good manners and the knightly traits of humor, courtesy, and generosity. Joshua worked hard on his family farm and grew up to be slim and muscular, handsome and tall, with piercing blue eyes. He learned to ride, to sail, and to fence with swords. He was a crack shot, but he hated killing animals. He loved poetry and played the piano and violin. Joshua eventually learned ten languages, including the language of the Aroostook Indians, who lived in birch-bark wigwams on his family's hundred-acre farm.

When he was thirteen, Joshua got the axle of a hay wagon stuck between two large rocks on his father's farm. With 400 pounds of hay on the wagon, the oxen could go neither forward nor back. Joshua's father ordered him to free the wagon and get it moving. When Joshua

asked, "How should I do it, Father?" his dad replied angrily, "Just do it!" With an act of superhuman strength that he didn't know he had, the young boy lifted the wagon, and the oxen started off with a jerk. No one was more surprised than Joshua, and the lesson stayed with him for life. From that day on, he had a sense that even the worst obstacles could be overcome with effort. A big problem he faced as a boy was an embarrassing stutter. But he worked hard to overcome it and eventually became a superb public speaker and even a professor of rhetoric!

Joshua's mother wanted him to be a minister, and his father hoped he would make a career in the army as had his grandfathers, both of whom had fought in the American Revolution. But Joshua felt trapped by all the rules and "petty despotisms" of both the ministry and the military. He loved ideas and the freedom to think and read, so he won a position as a professor at Bowdoin College, where he taught French, German, Greek, Latin, and Rhetoric. He married Fannie Adams, and the couple settled into a quiet college routine and eventually produced five children.

Joshua loved this life. But then Abraham Lincoln was elected president of the United States and threatened to abolish slavery. The slave states declared war and tried to split our country in two. Joshua hated slavery, which he would later call "a pox on the nation." And he loved America. When the Civil War began, Joshua knew he could not stay out of the fray. He wrote, "But, I fear, this war, so costly of blood and treasure, will not cease until the men of the North are willing to leave good positions, and sacrifice the dearest personal interests, to rescue our Country from desolation. . . . every man ought to come forward and ask to be placed at his proper post."* He left his family and Bowdoin College to volunteer for the Union army in 1862. He was thirty-four years old.

2.
LIEUTENANT COLONEL CHAMBERLAIN

✦

ALTHOUGH HE LACKED ANY MILITARY BACKGROUND, Joshua's strong education landed him the rank of lieutenant colonel in the newly formed 20th Maine Infantry Regiment. He worked hard to make himself a good leader. He read every manual and military history he could find and studied books about maneuvers and tactics by lantern in his tent, late into the night. Each day he drilled his men tirelessly, a routine that would save their lives and our nation at Gettysburg. "It is the discipline which is the soul of armies," he later said. "Other things—moral considerations, impulses of sentiment, and even natural excitement—may lead men to great deeds; but taken in the long run, and in all vicissitudes, an army is effective in proportion to its discipline."*

Joshua's men despised the constant drilling but idolized their lieutenant. Although officers were entitled to better food and conditions, Joshua cheerfully underwent the same hardships as his men. He slept

5

outdoors, using his saddle as a pillow and wrapping himself in a rubber blanket when it rained. When he ordered his men to do chores, such as building fortifications, he would strip off his shirt, pick up a shovel or ax, and work side by side with them.

3.
FREDERICKSBURG

JOSHUA'S REGIMENT LEFT MAINE, bound for Washington, where it joined the Union army. Joshua's first battle was the bloodiest day in American history. General Robert E. Lee's Confederate army had invaded the Union state of Maryland and was caught at Antietam on September 17, 1862. Joshua and his regiment, held in reserve, watched the terrible slaughter from the sidelines. More than 22,700 Americans, on both sides, were killed or wounded. The Union army suffered the most casualties, but General Lee was driven back into the South.

The Union army chased the Confederates across the Potomac River, catching them at Fredericksburg, Virginia. There, on December 13, 1862, the wily General Lee turned and dealt the bluecoats a terrible defeat. The 20th Maine was in the forefront of the battle.

More than 78,000 Confederates occupied the frozen high ground behind a stone wall near Fredericksburg. They were besieged by 115,000 Union troops. Because of a bungled battle plan, fourteen

Yankee regiments charged the Rebs, one at a time, and were mowed down. Not a single bluecoat ever reached the Confederate trenches. Joshua's horse was shot as he rode into the battle, and he was thrown into the Potomac. He was unharmed, but he and his men were trapped on the plain west of the city, where they fought all night behind a breastwork of bodies of their fallen comrades. Joshua was wounded when a musket ball grazed his neck and right ear. The next morning, the Union generals, seeing the hopelessness of their position, ordered their battered army to withdraw.

4.
GETTYSBURG

EMBOLDENED BY THIS VICTORY, General Lee again invaded the North the following summer, in 1863. General Lee wanted to capture a Northern city, such as Washington or Baltimore, and then force President Lincoln to sign a peace treaty allowing the Confederacy to secede. After marching for two days in crushing heat, mostly without food or sleep, the Union army caught Lee near a Pennsylvania village named Gettysburg.

Joshua's 20th Maine had only 238 of the 500 men that would comprise a full regiment. As the army assembled at Gettysburg, General George Gordon Meade delivered to him, at gunpoint, 120 mutineers from a disbanded Maine unit with orders that Joshua "make them do their duty or shoot them down."

After questioning the deserters, Joshua concluded they'd been badly mistreated. He promised to plead their case with the generals, and told them that if they followed him, he would treat them as soldiers should be treated. Inspired by his leadership and fairness, they turned out to be among his best fighters.

5.
LITTLE ROUND TOP

〜◆〜

EVEN AS THE UNION ARMY WAS ARRIVING AT GETTYSBURG, the Confederates launched their attack. Little did Joshua know that this day the fate of his nation rested on his shoulders. Joshua's corps commander, Colonel Strong Vincent, pointed to a hill named Little Round Top that overlooked Cemetery Ridge, where the Union army was digging in to make its stand. If the Confederate army took that hill, it could rain down artillery that would quickly destroy the Union forces. General Lee would then be able to conquer Washington, Baltimore, and Philadelphia. The South could win the Civil War. The Confederates had already swept over the neighboring hill, Big Round Top, and they were racing to occupy Little Round Top. Colonel Vincent ordered Joshua to "hold that ground at all hazards."

Joshua raced up Little Round Top on horseback beside his two brothers, Tom and John. Both brothers had followed Joshua's example and joined the Union cause. Tom was one of Joshua's twenty-eight junior officers, and John was serving as an army chaplain. As they rode, a Confederate cannonball missed them by only inches. Joshua ordered his brothers to separate. "Another such shot," he told them, "might make it a hard day for Mother."

Joshua narrowly beat the Confederates to the summit of Little Round Top. But before his men had the chance to dig in, the Confederates mounted a hot attack, hoping to capture the hill. As Joshua's soldiers took their positions, they were already being bombarded by cannons and picked off by sharpshooters. Rebel shells came screaming down upon them. A splinter of shrapnel tore through Joshua's boot, slicing his foot. When the Confederate cannonading finally stopped, there was an ominous silence, and Joshua knew the charge was coming.

Joshua had faith in his Maine men. Each of them understood the consequences of losing this hill to the Confederates. He saw the bravery and determination in their faces. His men knew that Joshua's calmness masked a heart of steel and the soul of a great warrior.

Then the terrifying howl of the Rebel yell rose above the roar of musket fire and electrified the air. The Confederate army fell heavily on the 20th Maine's entire line. Their first charge took the Rebels to ten feet from Joshua before a terrible hail of bullets from the 20th

Maine beat them back. The Confederates caught their breath, regrouped, and charged once more, battering Joshua's lines again and again with waves of desperate assaults. Sometimes they would drive Joshua's boys back a few yards, but each time, the 20th Maine would fight ferociously and regain the lost ground. For two full hours, the edge of the fight rolled backward and forward like a wave. To Joshua there seemed to be no end to the attacks. But he walked calmly up and down the line, giving his soldiers words of encouragement. Often, at great risk, he ventured out in front of his men to read the battlefield.

From this vantage, he spotted Confederate Colonel William Oates's Alabama regiment climbing stealthily around the hill through the underbrush to flank him on the left and attack his line from the rear. His long study of military history and tactics allowed him to quickly devise a plan to meet this attack. He ordered his troops to keep up rapid fire while sidestepping to the left between shots, extending his left line in a horseshoe to open up a new front at his rear. The constant drilling paid off. His men executed the complicated maneuver on the rough hillside terrain with energy, quickness, and precision that made even Joshua marvel. In a few minutes, the Confederates charged from their hiding places in the bushes with a bloodcurdling howl and rifles firing. But instead of meeting the undefended rear of Joshua's line, the Rebels encountered musket fire from Joshua's boys that tore their charge to pieces. Colonel Oates was shocked at the power of the Union defense, which he later described as "the most destructive fire I had ever seen."

Now greycoats were flooding the hill on all sides with fury. Through the gun smoke, Joshua saw the powder-blackened faces of his troops as they wrestled with Confederates in savage hand-to-hand fighting, cutting, thrusting, grappling, and firing their weapons at close range. Joshua saw "things that cannot be told or dreamed. All around, a strange mingled roar," he wrote, recalling the scene, "shouts of defiance, rally, and desperation; and underneath, murmured entreaty and stifled moans; gasping prayers, snatches of Sabbath song, whispers of loved names; everywhere men torn and broken, staggering, creeping, quivering on the earth, and dead faces with strangely fixed eyes staring stark into the sky. How men held on, each one knows—not I."* Sometimes there were more of the enemy around him than his own men. A decimating volley from the Confederate line knocked Joshua to the ground with a shot to his thigh. Fortunately, his metal sword scabbard diverted the bullet, and he rose again with a painful bruise.

But now he saw that the volley had cut a wide hole in the center of his line. Through the smoke, Joshua glimpsed the twenty-five-year-old color guard sergeant Andrew Tucker standing alone in the gaping breach, the flag braced against his shoulder. With his free hand, Tucker picked up a rifle from a fallen friend and began firing upon the graycoats who were charging him. Joshua ordered his brother Tom into the gap, knowing he might die there. When the smoke cleared, both boys were still standing, and the Rebels had withdrawn. During this short lull, Joshua ordered his soldiers to throw up a stone wall to protect themselves from the next assault. Their ammunition was nearly exhausted,

and the Maine soldiers scurried to gather the last remaining cartridges from their dead and wounded comrades.

Each Confederate attack seemed more intense than the last. During one assault, a Rebel sniper hiding behind a large boulder got Joshua clearly in his gun sights. Joshua's shoulder straps identified him as a lieutenant colonel, and the Rebel knew a Yankee officer would be a great trophy. Yet, when he squeezed his trigger, a strange feeling made him stop. Angry at himself for hesitating, he tried to pull the trigger again. Again he was unable to fire the deadly bullet, and he gave up. Joshua would not know till years afterward how narrowly he had escaped death.

As the beleaguered Maine soldiers divvied up their tiny store of bullets, the brave Confederates mounted their most ferocious assault of the day. With a final volley of concentrated fire, the 20th Maine drove the exhausted Rebels backward and down the hill. But now Joshua's boys were completely out of ammunition. Standing behind his thinning ranks, Joshua looked around. He watched the Confederates regather among the boulders and bushes for yet another attack. Joshua could see the effect of the repeated Confederate charges on his position. The situation looked grim. Half his men were dead or badly wounded. Some officers shouted that their units had been annihilated. The enemy forces outnumbered his by two to one. Without ammo, the shredded remains of his regiment had no hope of repulsing another attack. Colonel Strong Vincent, his commander, lay dying from a mortal wound far down the Union line on Cemetery Ridge. Joshua remembered Vincent's words: "Hold that ground at all hazards!" His desperate men looked back at him for orders. He would later remember that moment. *"My thoughts were running deep."* Suddenly, the solution occurred to him: since he was too weak to defend, he would attack!

He shouted the astounding command to "Fix bayonets!" The order flew from man to man down the line, along with the metal clash of bayonets being attached to empty rifles. Then a wild shout rose spontaneously from Joshua's desperate soldiers, and before he had a chance to shout "Charge," they were piling over the barricades and sprinting downhill toward the astonished Confederates. Brave as the Rebels were, the unexpected sight of 200 careening wild men thundering down upon them with blades of cold steel caused their courage to falter. Joshua's boys slammed into the Confederate lines with unstoppable momentum from their downhill charge, and the exhausted Confederates broke and flew in every direction or turned to raise their hands in surrender. Within minutes, Chamberlain's 200 men had taken 400 captives. Entire companies surrendered as one.

Dashing forward with his men, Joshua ran headfirst into a Confederate officer, who pointed a large navy revolver at Joshua's face and fired. Miraculously, the bullet only grazed Joshua's head. Joshua put his saber to the man's throat, and the greycoat immediately raised his hands in surrender. As Joshua took the officer's pistol, he was feeling exalted: the 20th Maine's downhill charge had broken the Rebel flank and ended the threat to Little Round Top.

6.
BIG ROUND TOP

FOLLOWING THEIR VICTORIOUS CHARGE, Joshua's men collapsed in exhaustion. But the battered survivors of the 20th Maine would neither celebrate nor sleep that night.

As twilight descended, the new corps commander, Colonel Rice, appeared at the 20th Maine's campfire. Rice, who had replaced Joshua's mortally wounded commander, Strong Vincent, had ordered another regiment to capture a neighboring hill known as Big Round Top, but its officer had refused. Frustrated, Colonel Rice was requesting—but not ordering—Joshua to perform the task. Joshua did not have the heart to command his exhausted troops into yet another fray. He told his boys, "I am going. As many of you men who feel able to do so can follow me." Then he turned, and with drawn sword, began limping up the hill on his wounded legs. Every man in the 20th Maine grabbed his musket to follow their colonel. Joshua ordered them to fix bayonets and creep quietly in the darkness. He feared that making noise would

reveal their small number to their enemy. Their stealth paid off. They surprised and captured a scouting party of twenty-five Rebels, along with a Confederate general. Baffled by the disappearance of their scouting party, the Confederate troops on Big Round Top assumed they were being surrounded by a much larger force, and fled downhill. By morning, Joshua had captured and fortified Big Round Top and received reinforcements so that it was firmly in Union control.

The Round Tops were the key to the whole battlefield at Gettysburg. The Confederates' failure to capture and keep them forced General Lee to make a full frontal attack on the center of the Union line the next day. Following Lee's orders, General George Pickett led approximately 15,000 gallant Confederates in a courageous but futile charge against Cemetery Ridge. Ten thousand graycoats died or were wounded. Pickett's Charge was the deadliest in the history of the American military. There were 51,000 casualties during the three days at Gettysburg—about as many Americans who were killed in action during the entire Vietnam war. That defeat put Lee into retreat and sapped the strength and spirit from the Confederate cause. Though the war would not officially end for two torturous years, Gettysburg was the beginning of the end for the Southern army, and Joshua Chamberlain's 20th Maine had set the stage for the Union victory.

7.
PETERSBURG

—◆—

AFTER ITS DEFEAT AT GETTYSBURG, the battered Confederate army escaped across the Potomac into the South. President Lincoln ordered General Ulysses S. Grant and his subordinate General George Meade to chase and destroy the Confederates. During the next year, Grant met Lee at many great battles across Virginia, including the Battle of the Wilderness in May, 1864, and the battles of Spotsylvania Court House and Cold Harbor later that month. In each battle, Joshua and his men fought bravely and often played important roles. Finally, the Confederate army holed up in the city of Petersburg, from which they could guard the road and rail lines to the capital of the Confederacy at Richmond. They erected strong fortifications and awaited attack.

Joshua stayed in touch with his family from the battlefield, writing long letters and short notes to Fannie and his children at every opportunity. "Dear Daisy, Do you and Wyllys have a pleasant time now-a-days? . . . How I should enjoy a May-walk with you and Wyllys, and what

beautiful flowers we would bring home to surprise Mamma and Aunty!
. . . I am suddenly ordered to go to the front to take command of our
pickets. Mamma will tell you what they are, so goodbye once more . . .
Papa."*

On June 18, 1864, General Meade ordered Joshua to lead the entire
Union army in a frontal assault against the heavily fortified city down a
valley called Rives' Salient. Surveying the landscape, Joshua had seri-
ous doubts about the planned attack. It meant charging across a long,
open, marshy field, crossing a stream, and climbing uphill without
cover, all within range of enemy guns. Joshua regarded the assignment
a death sentence and asked Meade to reconsider. When Meade
refused, Joshua grimly prepared to lead the attack.

Joshua drew his sword, ordered his men to charge, and began the
desperate dash toward 7,500 Confederate muskets that bristled over
tall Rebel fortifications mounted with powerful cannons.

The earth shook with the roar of guns, the din of shots, the screaming of horses and men. Exploding shells furrowed the ground. As
Joshua climbed from the creek, ahead of the army, he was shot
through by a minié ball. The bullet entered his right thigh and came
out his left hip, crushing his pelvis bone and piercing his bladder and
spleen. Not wanting his men to see him fall, he leaned on his sword
with desperate valor and remained standing until the first wave of the
charge moved past him. Then he collapsed. Joshua believed himself to
be dying, so when an ambulance crew came with a stretcher to retrieve
him, he ordered them to leave him where he lay and tend to the other

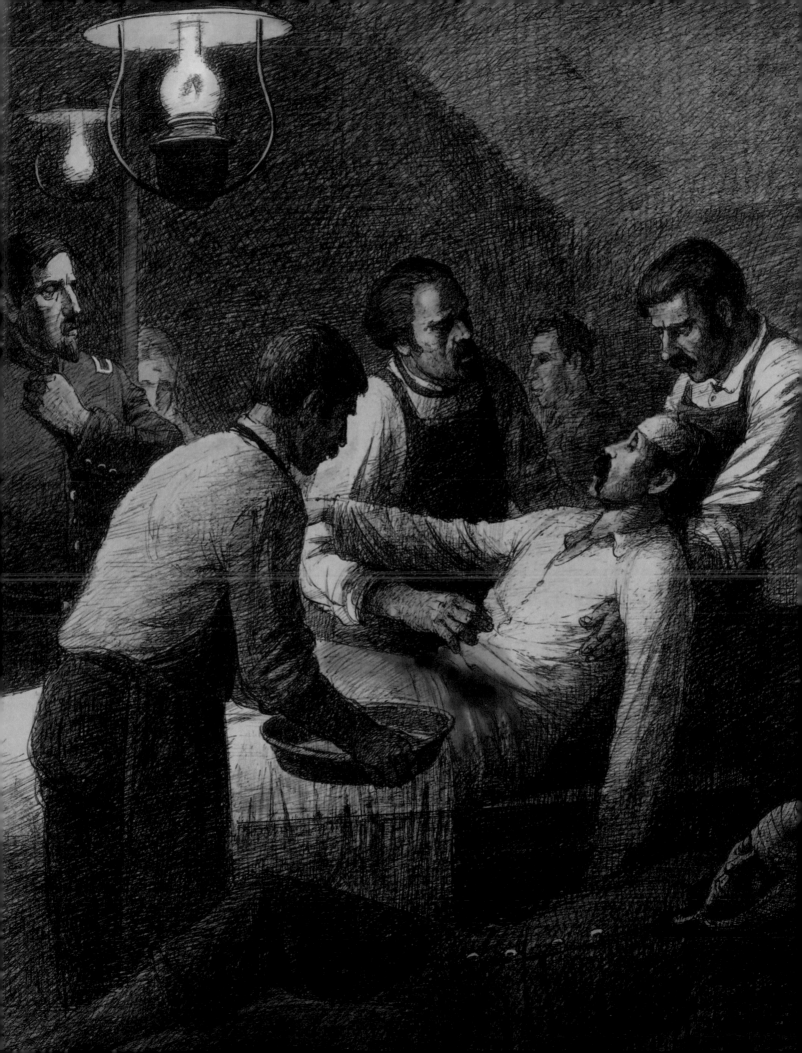

wounded. They ignored his order. At the field hospital, the surgeon said that Joshua could not survive. His officers and commanders gathered in the hospital tent to bid him good-bye. General Grant gave him a deathbed promotion to brigadier general. It was the only battlefield promotion that Grant ever gave. The newspapers printed Joshua's obituary.

But doctors cared for him in field tents and hospitals for five months, and, thanks to his unconquerable spirit and will to live, Joshua made a miraculous recovery. His wife and family begged him to retire from the army, but in November, though unable to walk a hundred yards or mount his horse unassisted, he reported for duty.

8.
VICTORY AT WHITE OAK ROAD

THE UNION CHARGE AT RIVES' SALIENT HAD, of course, failed, and the Union army began a one-year siege of Petersburg. In late March 1865, just after Joshua returned to his post, General Grant ordered a second attempt to take Petersburg. Joshua, now a brigadier general, again led the Union center. This time they would charge the Confederate fortification southwest of the city, along White Oak Road. Sword raised, Joshua ordered the charge. Charlemagne, his hot-blooded warhorse, smoking at a gallop, got well ahead of the troops. A bullet penetrated Charlemagne's neck and then passed through Joshua's bridle arm and slammed against his chest, knocking him unconscious. His life was saved only by a brass-backed field mirror in his breast pocket that prevented the shot from reaching his heart. The diverted bullet traveled around Joshua's body, inside his coat and out the back seam, striking Joshua's aide, Lieutenant Vogel, and knocking him off his horse. General Griffin galloped over to Joshua, who was slumped unconscious on

Charlemagne's neck. Griffin grabbed him around the hip to save him from falling. "My dear friend," he asked Joshua, "are you gone?"

Waking up at that moment and still groggy, Joshua thought General Griffin was asking him whether his charge had failed. He looked across the battlefield and saw that, sure enough, the Pennsylvania regiments on the army's right flank were in retreat before a Rebel counterattack. The Pennsylvania officers had been killed by a deadly volley of musket fire, and without leadership, the brave Pennsylvania veterans were fleeing. Without answering General Griffin, Joshua dashed off on the bleeding Charlemagne to shore up the line. Though he had no business in that part of the field, he flew toward the Pennsylvanians at full gallop down the center of the battlefield between the two armies. Bullets from both sides whizzed around him, and artillery shells pummeled the earth on every side. The ground shivered; dirt flew from Charlemagne's hooves; and a thousand Confederate infantrymen and sharpshooters fired their muskets at Joshua, hoping to knock the Yankee general off his horse.

When he reached the Pennsylvanians, Joshua, drenched in blood—his own and Charlemagne's—waved his sword wildly as he dashed back and forth before the Confederate lines, calling the retreating Pennsylvanians back to the battle. Inspired by this wild spectacle, the Pennsylvanians turned and rallied behind the bloodied general. They threw themselves savagely upon their attackers, driving the Rebels back behind their barricades.

Satisfied with this result, Joshua galloped back toward his proper position in the center of the line. As he rode across the battlefield, again in full view of both lines, the Union troops erupted in wild cheers for his spectacular show of courage. Then, for a moment, the battle stopped completely as Confederate soldiers climbed atop their barricades, doffed their hats, and joined the Yankees, loudly cheering the gallant Yankee general.

Back in place in the center, Joshua sent his wounded horse to the rear and continued to lead his men against the enemy on foot. Once again, he got ahead of his troops. In his excitement, Joshua crossed the Confederate lines and landed amid a group of Rebel soldiers, who surrounded him, pointing their rifles and demanding his surrender. Quick thinking saved Joshua from Confederate prison. Realizing that his battle-faded blue coat had been stained gray by gun smoke and dust, he pretended to be a Confederate general. Putting on his best Southern drawl, he shouted, "Surrender? Don't you see them Yankees upon us?" He waved his sword to signal his captors to follow him in a charge on the Yankees. Fooled by his accent, the Confederate soldiers followed Joshua into the hands of his men, and they were captured.

Joshua's actions at White Oak Road had turned a Union defeat into a resounding victory and broke the Confederate hold on Petersburg. He was promoted to the rank of major general for his gallantry.

In the next twenty-four hours, although wounded through the arm, Joshua would lead and direct his troops at three more battles, at Quaker Road, Gravely Run, and Five Forks, with no sleep: leading charges, enduring new wounds, crawling in the mud, dashing across

hot battlefields on foot and on horseback and capturing thousands of prisoners. At Five Forks, another horse would be shot out from beneath him. Union victories in these battles destroyed General Lee's flank and forced the Confederates to flee Petersburg. A reporter from New World Press who witnessed the battles called Joshua the "hero of Quaker Road, Gravely Run and Five Forks." Afterward, Joshua, now in charge of a division of 10,000 men, joined the pursuit of Lee's broken army.

9.
APPOMATTOX

FOR TWELVE DAYS OF FORCED MARCHES with little food or sleep, Joshua and his men chased Lee and his soldiers as the Confederates tried to flee to North Carolina. The bluecoats finally trapped Lee at Appomattox. There, in a narrow valley, the two armies faced each other: 110,000 Union soldiers against fewer than 28,000 ragged Rebels who could still fight for the South.

As Joshua surveyed the awesome scene, he saw three officers on horseback break from the Confederate lines and trot toward him, carrying a white flag of truce. When they got closer, he could see that their flag was a towel. They told Joshua that their army was ready to surrender, and that General Lee wanted to discuss terms with General Grant.

It was a stupendous moment. Joshua knew that five bloody years of war were finally ended. America was saved. Slavery was abolished. The cause for which he had suffered and risked his life and watched so many close friends die had been won. Joshua had survived and could now return to his family and his beloved state of Maine. Yet, all he could think about at that moment was to wonder, after months of continuous fighting in the mud, where in the world the Rebels had found that clean white towel.

After the terms of surrender were signed on April 9, General Grant chose Joshua to perform the task of accepting the formal surrender of the Confederate army on April 12, 1865. This was Grant's way of recognizing Joshua's bravery and the important role he had played in securing the Union victory. At the ceremony, Joshua took special care to spare the Confederates humiliation. It was a cool, wet day. The Union army formed lines on the road leading to Appomattox Court House to watch the ragged gray Confederate column trudge toward them to surrender. As the defeated Rebels lined up before him, Chamberlain called his men to attention and ordered them to salute their former enemies. At the head of the Confederate column, a sad General John Gordon heard the shifting of weapons and recognized the honor. He rose in his saddle, reined in his horse, and boldly returned the salute. Thanks to Joshua, the final act of the terrible war was a gesture of compassion and mutual respect. Tales of Joshua's kindness spread like wildfire in the South and made him very popular among his former foe.

After the war, Joshua returned to Maine to teach at his beloved Bowdoin College. In 1866, he was drafted by the Republican Party to run for governor of Maine. He was elected with the largest majority in the state's history and served four terms. He left politics to become president of Bowdoin College, and he died a hero in 1914 at the age of eighty-five.

Joshua was present at the second birth of our great nation. Indeed, he played a major role in the painful birthing process. Over the course of three years, he commanded troops in twenty-four battles and countless skirmishes. He was wounded six times. Six horses were shot out from under him. His soldiers captured 2,700 prisoners and eight battle flags. Before the war, this citizen soldier was a noble epitome of America's greatest virtues and the highest aspirations of mankind. During our nation's greatest crisis, he was a model for the courage, character, perseverance, and idealism that, for many generations, have defined the American people in the eyes of the world.

General Joshua L. Chamberlain, 1914

"The inspiration of a noble cause involving human interests wide and far, enables men to do things they did not dream themselves capable of before, and which they were not capable of alone. The consciousness of belonging, vitally, to something beyond individuality; of being part of a personality that reaches we know not where, in space and time, greatens the heart to the limits of the soul's ideal, and builds out the supreme of character."*

QUOTATION SOURCES

Quotations were taken from *In the Hands of Providence: Joshua L. Chamberlain and the American Civil War* by Alice Rains Trulock, University of North Carolina Press, 1992.

*Page 4: Excerpt from a letter to Governor Washburn, July 14, 1862

*Page 5: From a speech given by Chamberlain to the members of the army of the Potomac Association, 1869

*Page 15: From "Through Blood and Fire at Gettysburg," a collection of Chamberlain's private Civil War papers, first published in *Hearst's Magazine* in 1913

*Page 24: Excerpts from a letter to Chamberlain's seven-year-old daughter Daisy, May 1863

*Page 37: From "The State, the Nation, and the People," an address given at the dedication of the 20th Maine Monuments at Gettysburg, October 3, 1889

BIBLIOGRAPHY

Foote, Shelby. *The Civil War: A Narrative, Vol.1, Fort Sumter to Perryville.* New York: Random House, 1958.

————. *The Civil War: A Narrative, Vol. 2, Fredericksburg to Meridian.* New York: Random House, 1963.

————. *The Civil War: A Narrative, Vol. 3, Red River to Appomattox.* New York: Random House, 1974.

Longacre, Edward G. *Joshua Chamberlain: The Soldier and the Man.* New York: Da Capo Press, 2003.

SUGGESTED READING

Shaara, Jeff. *Jeff Shaara's Civil War Battlefields: Discovering America's Hallowed Ground.* New York: Random House, 2006.

Shaara, Michael. *The Killer Angels.* New York: David McKay Publications, 1974.